The 12-Mi
B

C000196669

How to Start
(a book, business or creative project)
When You're Stuck

Practical inspiration to get
your idea off the ground

Robbie Swale

Winds of Trust Publications

Contents

Part One: ONLY START

Part Two: HOW TO START

Part Three: WHY START?

Our inspiration is always there, but it's at the moment when we commit to something and make the start that we let inspiration in.

One thing we can be sure of is that nothing we want to create will exist unless we start it.

Impact

'I was paralysed by fear and indecision until I came across Robbie's work. Now, thanks to the 12-Minute Method, I believe that I am an author and I am writing my first book.'
Nadine Kelly, M.D.,
Founder of YOGI M.D.

'Robbie's writing and 12-Minute Method inspired me to finally take the first steps to start a business I'd had in my mind (and done nothing about) for years. Learning to lean into resistance and just take the first step has had a huge impact on my mindset, mental health, family and career development. In the four years since, we have become a successful, award-winning business! I'm extremely grateful to Robbie for his genuinely impactful and thought provoking 12-minute articles.'
Paul Thompson
Founder/Health and Wellbeing Coach and Consultant, WorkSmart Wellbeing

'I wouldn't have written any of what I have without Robbie's example and his 12-minute approach. It's what gave me the initial courage to try such a writing practice myself, to break through both fear and creative blockage... and then to post one article, then several, then to become known for such writing. When someone mentioned I should write a book, the only thing that gave me the confidence to believe I could was seeing what Robbie had already accomplished. I am on page 316 of my flash draft.'

Peter Tavernise
Leadership Coach

'As a true believer in the power of creativity to fire us up and get us into action, I see Robbie as a real leader in the field. His ability to excite and inspire even the most reluctant participants is really impressive. Whether in academia, tech, finance, culture or anything in between, Robbie will help you put aside the noise and focus on what is really important to you.'

Jo Hunter
Co-Founder and CEO, 64 Million Artists

'The ethos of the 12-Minute Method is inspiring and challenging, but it is hearing what led Robbie to it in the first place that connects most. Words matter, but so does the spirit and story behind the words, and that's what catches me more than anything about Robbie's writing.'

Dr Hannah Mather
Executive Coach, Theologian, and Author, The Interpreting Spirit

'Many times, in many ways, I have recommended the 12-Minute Method to others and watched them come alive with inspiration when they hear how Robbie brought this book to life. His genius ideas are exponentially valuable. To me, it's the 12-Minute Miracle.'

Michelle C. Basey
Energy Healing Artist and CoreYou Coach

'I would highly recommend Robbie to anyone who is facing what feels like an insurmountable hurdle, whether it's personal or professional.'

Emma Kerr
Senior Global Practice Specialist, DAI

'Robbie will get an acknowledgment in my second book, as he did in my first. The second couldn't have been written without the first and my first would never have been written without Robbie's leadership and his 12-Minute Method. His fingerprints are forever more on anything I publish! Robbie's guidance will support your progress and will lead you to share the 12-Minute Method with others. It's that good.'

David W. Reynolds
Creator and host of the Lead. Learn. Change. Podcast;
Author, Lead. Learn. Change

'I've always liked to write. However, I'm not a writer. Why would I write, if I'm not a writer? Stumbling upon Robbie's 12-Minute Method gave me permission to write. Anyone can be a writer for 12 minutes! Since incorporating the method into my weekly routine, and publishing on social, I am considered by many to be a "thought leader" in my space.'

Bryon Howard

CEO, The Howard Team Real Estate Services – eXp Realty

'"Surely I can find 12 minutes in a day," I thought when I saw Robbie's workshop on "how to write a book in 12 minutes". It was a low barrier to entry towards creating a sustainable writing practice. It was the best decision I have made. I have now published a book and have been writing for 483 consecutive days. I would not have done that had it not been for Robbie's idea, but more importantly seeing him walk his talk with the 12-Minute Method.'

Karena de Souza

Author, Contours of Courageous Parenting

'Each time I talk with Robbie, he gives me a new thought to think about.'

Robert Holden

Author, Authentic Success

'Whatever progress you wish you could make in your career, or more generally in your life – whether it's starting a business, writing your first book, or any other new beginning – Robbie's 12-Minute Method will help you overcome the obstacles in your way, focus your energy and start!'

Alex Swallow

Author, How To Become An Influencer

About The Author

Written on 13th October 2021

I'm Robbie Swale, a writer and coach.

There have been many times in my life where I didn't get my ideas off the ground, where I was stuck in creative hell and where I wasn't productive. Thankfully, mostly that has changed.

Now people call me prolific and that's all down to the lessons I learned while creating the 12-Minute Method. Some of the things I have beaten procrastination to do and finally got off the ground include:

- A blog, clocking in at over 200 articles; each written in 12 minutes
- A coaching business, built from nothing, that could support me full-time in less than two years
- *Aprendiendo español* (I've got a long way to go, but I'm moving and not stopping)
- A website dedicated to my favourite author, now containing over 300 inspirational snippets of wisdom (read more at **www.wisdomofgemmell.com**)
- A podcast, including interviews with best-selling authors and world-famous coaches (**www.thecoachsjourney.com**)

- Books: this one, three more due out in 2022, and another that's almost finished
- A career change
- Getting married

I spent the first decade of my career doing lots of different things. I was a director, a trustee, a manager, almost a professional actor, a leader and an administrator.

In my current work, I'm interested in three things:

Creativity (and why people don't do the things they want to do).

Leadership and how people can be honourable in their work. How they can find success without feeling like they have to compromise their values and identity.

Coaching: the amazing craft that allows each of us to develop vital skills for our future and to more often be our wisest and most skilful selves.

I've coached people working on amazing creative ideas, from businesses to books and beyond. I've worked with people on many incredible projects that you will never have heard of. I've also worked, coached, trained and facilitated for organisations like Swiss Re, the University of Edinburgh, the Royal Opera House, Moonpig, UCL and more.

I'm proud to be an associate of 64 Million Artists, an organisation dedicated to unleashing the creativity of everyone in the UK, and a Fellow Coach for BetterUp, the world's biggest mental health and coaching organisation.

Mostly, though, I'm proud that I've felt fear, felt resistance, felt the pull of procrastination, and I've battled it, knowing that that battle was a battle for my soul: to take me out of creative hell and grow me into someone new. There have been many ideas that haven't made it because I didn't know how to fight that battle. But my line is drawn: *not anymore.*

Read more about me and sign up to my mailing list at:

www.robbieswale.com

About This Book

This is a book about how to get unstuck and get started.

It's about *that* thing.

You know the one.

The one you've been meaning to do; the one you wish you'd done.

It's about how to get that thing off the ground, so that a year from now it's out in the world, not still rattling around in your head.

This book is not a 'how to guide' in the traditional sense. There are no 'six steps to start your business'. There is no exact map to follow. No 'go here and you will get this'.

The creative process – the process of making something from nothing – is too complex for that. You need to find the unique mix of inspiration, ideas and practices that work *for you*.

Read this book looking for the ideas that will help *you*. It probably won't be all of them, but it certainly won't be none of them.

Something here will help you to stop being a frustrated creative or a frustrated entrepreneur, and start being an active creative or entrepreneur.

Something here will be exactly what you need to get your idea off the ground.

That idea could be a book you've always wanted to write, a business you want to start, a habit you want to make part of who you are…

It could be making a change to your career, creating and releasing an album, or making a change to a relationship in your life…

It could be pretty much anything that you want to be different about your life now and how you live it.

Sound ambitious? Maybe, but that's how powerful the 12-Minute Method can be.

To find that something (or somethings) you need, you first need to take charge of how you use this book. As you read, look for the spark that motivates you in each chapter, each section. When you find it, think about how you're going to use it. Sometimes a single spark is all it takes to light the fire.

If you would like some help keeping track of the sparks, you can download a ready-made worksheet to help you design your own 12-minute practice here:

www.robbieswale.com/12minute-method-downloads

This book is organised into easily digestible, bite-size sections, so you can dip into it wherever you want and skip about liberally, if that is what works best for you.

Or, you can scan through the contents, find a chapter title that speaks to you today, then read it, trusting that you'll be guided to the insight you need to hear in this particular moment.

Or, finally, you can read it from cover to cover if that feels right. I put it together to be read in that manner, with an energy and arc from beginning to middle to end.

Above all, remember that everything that was made, at some point was nothing. Everything that exists, at some point needed to be started.

So, let's start.

Robbie Swale

August 24, 2021

The 12-Minute Method

The 12-Minute Method emerged from my struggles. Setting out on a new journey, into a new part of my life, I was looking at myself deeply for the first time. And I noticed something. I was scared – *really scared* – of sharing anything of myself online. I hadn't always been that way, but in 2016, I was. Yes, I was scared of sharing anything I had created, but even of sharing a post on Facebook. It filled me with anxiety, causing tension to rise in my chest.

More important to me than social media though was creating things. I hadn't always held myself back when creating things, but for the years leading up to 2016, I had. I was very aware that two great ideas had passed me by, moving on in the way Liz Gilbert describes in *Big Magic*, to someone else. The chance for me to be the person who had made them was gone. And I didn't want that to happen again.

But more important to me than missing out on ideas was that *I wanted to create*. I wanted to share myself with the world. So, I took this fear to my coach at the time, Joel Monk, and gradually, things shifted. I shared a poem I had written, then a longer article. But the real shift, the thing that made all the difference for me, the moment that really marked the start of the 12-Minute Method, happened when

Joel shared that in his previous career as a visual artist, he had liked to create series of paintings. What if, he asked, I created a series of articles?

We had spoken about how I valued the time I had to myself on my short train journey from Clapham Junction to Waterloo each day, so we designed a practice to overcome my fear of sharing myself online, and to allow me to create something. Here was the practice:

Write on the train. Start when the train starts moving, stop when the train stops. Then, proofread it once and share it online. No time to get in my own way. Just time to write and share.

We agreed that I would do this five times over the next two weeks. This was important, partly because it was a way to make sure I didn't give up if the first one terrified or embarrassed me too much. I chose to post them on LinkedIn, because I thought no one really read LinkedIn.

After posting five articles, however, I noticed something was happening. People – a handful of people, but real people nonetheless – had responded warmly to those five pieces. I went on holiday after those five pieces, with that feedback and the experience of writing and sharing them in my mind. When I got back, I committed to writing one article each week from then on. One per day or five every two weeks felt like too many. But one article on my train journey every week, I could do.

After a while, my circumstances changed and I didn't need to take the train daily anymore, so I checked how long the journey took the next time I travelled from Waterloo to Clapham Junction. It took 12 minutes.

So, on weeks when I didn't get the train, I would set a timer for 12 minutes.

I would write when the timer was going, stop when the timer stopped. Proofread it once and post it on LinkedIn. Once a week. As I write this, that practice has been going now for five years and one week.

Strangely, the train from Clapham Junction to Waterloo (or back) almost never lasts *exactly* 12 minutes. Often, it's 8 or 9 or 11. A few times a day it lasts 12 minutes though, so here we are: *The 12-Minute Method.*

Gradually, as the practice continued, I realised that something was happening as I wrote the pieces – something quite powerful.

First, I began to see that I was *changing* through this practice; my sense of "Who I am" was being changed.

Second, something was being *created.*

And a pattern was emerging.

As I'll describe in *Chapter 1 – It's Time To Start*, I saw this pattern clearly three times in my own life – then I began to see it elsewhere. The 12-minute writing practice had exposed a truth about human experience that, somehow, I'd never known. Not knowing it had held me back from being better, and doing more, in almost every aspect of my life. That truth is this:

If you start something and do it regularly – even for only 12 minutes each week – and keep doing it, after a few years you'll have something – and it might be something magical.

That is the essence of the 12-Minute Method.

Around two and a half years into this practice, I received an email from author and marketing thought-leader Seth Godin, publicising a compilation of his blog, published as a book. I bought it as a treat for myself and loved it, even though I had read many of Godin's articles and books already. This gave me an idea: maybe I could turn my 12-minute articles into a book. I could even call it something funny like, *I Wrote This Book in 12 Minutes.*

I shared the idea with my friend, Steve, planning to enlist his copyediting skills to help with the new book. Steve pointed out that the power of the title was that it would empower people to create something, even in as little as 12 minutes each week. In other words, 'I wrote this book 12 minutes at a time. If I can do that, what can you do?'

But then he asked, could the content of the book help people with that too? Not just the method with which it was written, but the advice the book would contain. I sat down and read the first three years of those articles, each written in 12 minutes, and it turned out that it could.

For the three years I had been writing those pieces – the pieces that make up this book and its sequels – I had been wrestling with how to release my own creative potential. I had been wrestling with how to do the things I wanted to do when I was scared, struggling and all over the place.

During this time, I had also begun working as a coach, helping others get out of their own way and achieve the things they wanted to achieve. Helping people understand why they didn't do the things they wanted to do, and helping them do those things. Throughout all of that, I had been writing in an *emergent* way: sit down, start writing, see what emerges.

And what emerged was, of course, what I was interested in, what I was thinking about. They were the ideas, insights, inspiration, practices and actions that could help people do the things they wanted to do, even – or especially – when they were stuck.

So, almost by accident, I had written not just *any* book, but a book about something specific. A book about wrestling with creative potential, about doing the things we want to do but are scared of, struggling with or all over the place about. And I had written it 12 minutes at a time.

What had emerged from my experimentation, learning, reading and work with clients was the second part of the 12-Minute Method: four key areas that each of us *have* to work on if we want to create something that makes a difference. Each of these is an area where I had fallen down and struggled, and where I had seen others fall down and struggle.

First, we have to start. We can't make anything if we don't start. Yet I had failed to start so many different things over the years.

Second, we have to keep going. In some ways this is the hardest bit. It means starting over and over again, not letting things slip. At some point, all of us have given up on things in our lives before we should have.

Third, if we want to do really great work, we have to create the conditions for that to happen. We can't control creativity, we can't control much in the complexity of the modern world, and we certainly can't control when we make something that feels truly great, truly magical. But we can do things that make us more likely to create something; more likely to do great work.

If I sit down every week for 12 minutes and write, at some point I'm going to write something really good. Not every time, but sometimes. There are other things we can do too, to make ourselves more prone to accidentally doing great work. These include relationships, ways of thinking, habits and more. The things that create the conditions for us to do our best work.

Finally, we have to share our work. At least, we do if we want to make a difference to people beyond ourselves. And the sharing, as my story shows, can feel like the hardest part. And it can be the most transformative.

This is what the practice of the 12-Minute Method does. It combines these four elements to get you unstuck and keep you unstuck:

1. Start

2. Keep going

3. Create the conditions for great work

4. Share your work

And the order matters. Starting is the start. That might sound silly, but 'create the conditions for great work' is a minefield of chances to get stuck: I'll start when my writing space is ready... I'll start when my office is set up... I'll start when my inbox is clear... I'll start when my kids go to school... That's all procrastination and resistance. In fact, in many ways, creating the conditions for great work is the *least* important part of this four-step process. The conditions are already better than you think, and they will never be perfect, so you can't wait for that perfection to start. First, as part one of this book says, *Only Start*.

As I worked on the book, provisionally titled *I Wrote This Book in 12 Minutes,* I realised that to allow the work to reach the largest number of people, to have the biggest impact, it might work better as a series. Four books, each covering one of those areas. What you are reading is the first part of that series, and it concerns the first part of the 12-Minute Method: *starting*.

This book comprises a selection of pieces, each written in 12 minutes, drawn from the first three years of that 12-minute writing practice. They are here to help inspire you, to show you that you are not alone and, most of all, to help you start.

Each of them is imperfect. Riddled with worry, as I sometimes am, it has been a painful, sometimes excruciating process to share them in this way. It is equally difficult to write this introduction, knowing that it will be imperfect; knowing I won't be able to capture *exactly* what I want to share, exactly the perfect thing to explain this book and these ideas to you. But I have to share it this way, because *I have to share it*. That's the fourth part of the 12-Minute Method and I know it's vital.

While the chapters in this book are not perfect, I know they are good enough to make a difference; good enough that they might just contain the spark you need to start something special.

Because the world needs what you have to create.

If there's one thing I feel sure of in the strange world in which we live – simultaneously seeming to be the best time ever to be alive, while also constantly teetering on the brink of disaster – it is that we need to realease the creative potential of as many people as possible to make this world a better place.

Your idea could do that. It may not feel like that, but it could. And we won't know unless you make it a reality.

But probably that's not what you're thinking of now. You probably just want to be out of the living hell of having an idea inside you, knowing you should do something with it, knowing you have the potential to do something with it, and yet still not doing it.

Maybe you have a whole pile of ideas, each burning a hole in the back of your mind. That's what life was like for me. That's what untapped creativity and unused ideas can feel like. Hell. That's how I hope this book will help you: I hope it will take you out of the hell of not doing the things you know deep down you want to do.

So, please use the 12-Minute Method and the ideas, actions and practices contained in the following pages to start *that thing*. You know the one.

Once you've started, even if it's just for 12 minutes each week, you will begin to change.

And in the months and years to come… who knows? You might even create something magical.

Free 12-Minute Method Action Sheet

I want your idea to get off the ground and to help you do that, I've created a worksheet that guides you through creating your own 12-minute practice and gives you somewhere to turn the insights you get from this book into action.

It also includes some recommended further reading from the thinkers and authors who have influenced this book, whose names you'll find in the chapters that follow.

You can download the action sheet for free at:
www.robbieswale.com/12minute-method-downloads
or by scanning this QR code:

Part One: ONLY START

First, only start.

Don't worry about how, why, where and when your creation will be out in the world. If, at the moment, all of that stuff feels impossible to work out, that's okay. You're human, after all. Remember: *when you start, inspiration appears.*

Every day you don't start means there will be another morning when you will wake up having done nothing about your idea. If you start today, tomorrow will be easier. If you start today, then tomorrow you will have something. You will have made something. You will be on the road. Maybe not far down it, but you will be travelling.

If you start today, then keep going, then in days or weeks or months you will have something. Something you can hold. Something you can be proud of.

But don't worry about that, today.

Don't let your thinking or your ego or your worries or your grand plans get in the way.

Starting. Starting is all that matters.

For today, only start.

Chapter One

It's Time to Start

Written on 5th October, 2017

It seems impossible. A massive task. So much to do. I'm so far behind. It'll take me forever. Forever. How can I start now, when so many people are so far ahead? What's even the point?

These are the things I used to think; questions I'd ask myself.

I thought those thoughts about the Wisdom of David Gemmell, the website I made about the wisdom and philosophy threaded through the work of the fantasy novelist. Then some coaching from my friend Inga Umblija and the work of Steven Pressfield and Seth Godin convinced me that if just one person read it, it would be worth it, and I didn›t have to have *exactly how* I would do it sorted at the start.

Then I just started, creating a database of entries on the website one week at a time, sending out tweets one day at a time. And now there are over 100 amazing pieces of wisdom and philosophy on the website, over 1,000 on Twitter, and hundreds of followers and sign-ups. Not that many in the grand scheme of things, but they love it, and it makes me proud.

I thought those thoughts with coaching, too.

I remember the first consultations I did with potential clients so clearly. I couldn't believe they'd signed up. And although I thought, 'Can I really start a new career *again,* a decade into my working life?' and although I compared myself to people who were better prepared for a career in coaching, or who had already done an impossible sounding 'hundreds of hours', I was convinced, by my own thinking and advice from my brother, Ewan Townhead, that the coach training would be valuable for me whatever I chose to do, as a career or not.

Now I have coached hundreds of people for hundreds of hours; it's the only work I do, and I'm much better at it than anything I've done before.

I thought those thoughts about writing. I had a strange pull in me to share myself more, but was distracted by worries. I remember how I posted those first pieces of writing. The anxiety and resistance and all the questions were there. In the end, the pieces were posted. And I kept posting. And now I've written over 60 pieces on LinkedIn, one at a time.

Now people say to me, 'You write a lot, don't you?'

No, I think, *I just play around with writing once a week.* But they're right. And that happened one article at a time.

Now people say to me, 'You've been doing this coaching thing a long time now, I'm just a beginner.'

No, I haven't, I think. ***I'm a beginner.*** But I'm not. And it changed one hour at a time.

I didn't mean to be a writer. I just started writing, because I felt the call to share myself. Then I wrote, one thing at a time, over several years. And now I am.

I kind of meant to be a coach. I thought it might be good. I thought I might be good at it. I was full of doubt. But I started, and coached one week at a time, one person at a time. And now I am.

I meant to create something about David Gemmell because I love his work. I really wanted to, for several years. But I almost didn't. And in the end, I did it one e-drop of wisdom at a time. And now I have created it. And it is there for as long as I want it to be.

I did this through good and bad, light and dark, doubt, and the burning knowledge that I knew I wanted it. I did it because people believed in me and helped me. I did it because it was important.

What is important to you?

What are you called to?

What are you called by?

It's time to start.

Chapter Two

Give Yourself the Permission You Need

Written on 13th December, 2017

I was on a call with a client last week and something came to me:

'It seems like you're waiting for permission for something. What do you want permission for?'

From there, things opened up.

We all wait for permission, but the *need* to wait is disappearing in the internet age. Seth Godin writes about how the gatekeepers are no more. No more do we *need* the permission of publishers (or anyone) to publish our book. We can just put it on Amazon. No more do we *need* the permission of TV executives (or anyone) to create our own daily, weekly, even hourly show. We can just post it on YouTube. We don't need the permission of a newspaper editor (or anyone) to publish the news as we see it, or to share opinion pieces and comments.

As Seth says, anyone with $100 and an internet connection can start a business now. You don't need a bank loan, or anything else. You could probably do it with less.

And yet we wait.

We haven't got used to it yet. Maybe the next generation will… or the next.

We wait for permission.

Sometimes we wait for approval, from ourselves or others. Perhaps a stamp of approval from a governing body, or a boss, or a partner, or a parent. Perhaps a feeling of permission: I'll start when I feel ready. That *feeling* is the permission I need.

Maybe it's the relic of an education system. Maybe it's the relic of the times when the internet didn't exist and you really did have to win the gatekeeper's approval to be a writer or an entrepreneur.

But it's time to stop waiting. Because it's slowing us down, everywhere, from creating the world we want to. How many great businesses haven't been started because people didn't get the permission they thought they needed? How many great songs are unpublished?

How many changes in organisations, which might have untold impact on hundreds or thousands of employees, or thousands or millions of customers, haven't been made because someone didn't have 'permission'?

Sometimes this is a real permission: employees hamstrung from creating change, heads of departments forbidding it.

But often it is just, 'It isn't my job…' or, 'If it was a good idea, someone else would have done it…' or 'Who am I to create change?'

But what if everyone is thinking that? What if everyone is sitting there waiting for permission? Permission to go the extra mile with a customer. Permission to go to the gym at lunchtime. Permission to change the structure of the organisation. Permission to add definition to a role, or take it away.

These decisions, and many more, are the things that will change the way we live, one person's world at a time.

I was able to give my client the permission she needed. I just told her that I was giving her it. We can all do that to the people we know. Give them the permission they need. Give it to them explicitly and implicitly, but give it.

I give you permission, now.

And we can do it for ourselves. Where in your life are you waiting for permission right now?

Give yourself the permission you need.

Right now.

And then get on with it.

Chapter Three

The Second-Best Time is Now

Written on 15th April, 2019

I wish, I thought to myself, sitting at my desk in my office job – my day job, midway through a career change and with a mind full of tangled string – *that I'd been keeping LinkedIn up to date this whole time.*

It felt excruciating to have to add people from 10 years ago, who I had met twice, as I desperately tried to understand and update my network in case it might help with whatever came next.

In the end, gradually, I added them. The ones I felt least embarrassed about first, then the next least embarrassing, through to some people who had almost certainly forgotten me. I didn't die. No one told me to get lost. Some people ignored me. No one laughed at or mocked me.

It was only much later that I realised how devious that wishing is. That wishing for time travel, for yesterday, when you could have started but didn't. That wish that you had started when you were young, when there was more time ahead of you, when you wouldn't be so far behind.

It holds you. It makes you think it's not worth trying to start. It makes you never add those people on LinkedIn, because you should have done it years ago. If you're lucky, what it does is make you never add those people.

But if you're unlucky, the price you pay may be years of not taking the leap and pursuing your calling.

Years of never asking out that person, the one who makes your stomach tingle and your mouth get tangled.

Years when you could have been teaching instead of working in this company you fell into.

Years you could have stayed in a relationship if you had *just started listening* to her, instead of giving it up as lost.

Years of not writing or not painting.

Years when you haven't been playing football or tennis.

Years where you haven't learned to play the piano, years without guitars, years without singing lessons, years without dance.

Years of sitting, listening to yourself, noticing that you're not happy. But you could be, if you chose to.

Years without taking responsibility for yourself, for your family, for the children you left behind.

Years without finding out how to love others and love yourself.

Years without giving up smoking, without getting into shape.

Years without saying, 'I'm not afraid of you anymore.'

Years of putting up, or settling, without inspiration and possibility.

Years without saying, 'Enough. I've had enough.'

I only know two Chinese proverbs. One of them is this:

The best time to plant an apple tree was twenty years ago. The second-best time is now.

The thing about wishing – that insidious wishing – is that the weight of it only grows, as each day, week, month or year passes. Every year you wait, it gets bigger.

The best time was whenever you wish you'd started.

The second-best time is now.

Chapter Four

'Clarity' and 'Knowing Enough'

Written on 16th December, 2016

Many of you know the feeling. I've had it this week. The world is pressing in on you. Wherever you put your thoughts, whichever part of your life you focus them on, there's a rising feeling. If you're lucky it's just worry, but maybe it's panic.

It can be about the pressures of your day-to-day life; it can be about where on earth your life is going. Sometimes it feels like it's nothing at all: it's just something unreachable, which makes things that are normally manageable (or even fun or exciting) impossible to deal with.

It's often this feeling which leads so many of us to seek 'clarity'. It's a word I hear often with clients. It's their aim for our work together: to gain more *clarity*. About an area of their life. About a decision they need to make. About where they want to get to.

And this week, it got me thinking: why are we obsessed with clarity?

Often, worry and panic come from a line of thought that goes, 'I don't know enough here.' And I wonder if that is an historical, evolutionary drive.

I've noticed I don't get the feeling as much on clear days. Or when I walk by the River Thames. Doing that actually *gives* me clarity. I've just moved into a flat on the ninth floor of a block in Battersea, south London. When I look out of the windows, especially on a clear day, that feeling of 'I don't know enough' seems to dissipate.

I heard once that growing up in a big city like London can have a psychological effect on children and young people, because they never see a horizon.

It strikes me that thousands of years ago, if you could see the horizon, then you would 'know enough'. About any dangers that might be nearby. About where food (which would have been a constant worry) could be found. If the day was clear, you would be even more likely to know enough. And if the water was clear, you would know enough about whether to get in it, whether you might find food in there, whether you could drink it.

Knowing enough – and the clarity to be sure you do – is an evolutionary drive for safety. No wonder we panic when we don't have it.

But that word 'enough'… it's dangerous.

You already know enough. You maybe just haven't realised it yet. But I'm confident you do. You're doing great.

Chapter Five
Two Rules for Possibility: Always be Early and Always Start

Written on 16th July, 2018

This morning I looked at my watch. Looked at the amount of time I had before I needed to leave, and slowed down. I thought, *To be safe, to make sure I'm on time, I still have time to do one thing. But just one.*

I chose the thing and did it. It took four minutes less than I thought, so I replied to another email thinking, *I can do this and still be on time.* But I couldn't. It took longer. The margin I'd allowed for something to go wrong was used up, so that when something did, I was suddenly running late. Now I'm sweating on a train, behind schedule.

It is painful to always be late, to be rushing, and to leave something we thought we could do unfinished.

Humans are terrible at understanding time.

To paraphrase a brilliant thought I heard from Tony Robbins, we always overestimate what we can achieve in short periods of time (days, weeks, maybe months or even one year; this is why our to-do lists never get finished), and we grossly underestimate what we can achieve in longer periods of time (think 1 year, 2 years, 5 years, 10 years).

These pieces of writing, written in 12 minutes (less today because it took me a couple of minutes to settle down after rushing for the train) are an exercise in possibility. I started by doing five and then continued, one per week, until there are nearly 100. One 12-minute piece of writing at a time.

I recently discovered that fantasy novelist Peter V. Brett is another train writer, creating vast swathes of his first novel on the New York subway, on his phone.

The possibility of what we can achieve is on my mind this week because it was three years ago on Saturday that someone paid me to coach them for the first time. At the time, I could barely believe it. Now there are many people I have coached, and the number of hours ticks up every week – one hour or half-hour at a time.

And it is tragic to think of all the things that are never started – blogs, novels, businesses, career changes, paintings, fitness programmes – because they seem too big.

Here are two rules to live by:

Always be early. I learnt this from an American football coach, via Ros Zander in her book *Pathways to Possibility*. It's almost impossible to be exactly on time: it's an exercise in squeezing things in, walking just a bit faster or a bit slower. It's unpleasant and you almost always fail. Being early, now that's something you can succeed at (although it's not necessarily easy, and I certainly haven't got it down yet). The *timeframe* of possibility then, is *always be early*.

Always start. That's all you need to do. Big dreams, small steps. Trust that when you start, and decide to keep starting day after day, time will become your ally in creation, not your enemy. Years will pass and you will have created a body of work you can be proud of. The *practice* of possibility then, is *always start*.

Chapter Six
To Me, By Me, Through Me

Written on 11th May, 2017

I haven't slept well the last couple of days. At first I put it down to an unsettling shift in the main character (and an uplift in the levels of tension and action) of the novel I've been reading: *The Painted Man* by Peter V. Brett. I love fantasy novels and reading before bed is one of the great pleasures in my life.

But today, I think it's something different. I think something is changing for me. It's not surprising this is the case. I recently became a full-time coach and in becoming fully self-employed, some of my identity has to shift. We hang so much of our identity on the work we do, and I am also now someone who can not only start a business, but make it work.

And two more things have changed this week. I have stepped up my involvement at The Coaching School, where I will be putting more time into helping them develop their brilliant organisation. And I published an article, about all the learning I have done over the past two years. I think it is these two things (more than Arlen's shift to becoming the Painted Man) which have led to this different feeling in me.

Jim Dethmer, a leadership coach and trainer, refers to three different ways of engaging with the world.

Life Happening To Me – where you are a victim of the occurrences and events of the world.

Life Created By Me – where you see yourself as the author of your life, creating and making things happen in the way that you want. And,

Life Happening Through Me – where you get out of the way and let things emerge through you, out into the world.

(There is actually one more: *Life Happening As Me*, but I don't quite understand that one… yet!)[1]

I have felt the call of this third stage, *Through Me*, for the last few months. Now I feel the *Through Me* experience calling even more, more than I have for a long time. Ideas to help The Coaching School keep popping into my head, with a feeling of intensity and excitement. I just need to be given permission (by myself and others) to have these ideas, then suddenly there they are, emerging through me.

It was the same writing the article about my learning from the last few years.[2] It had a life of its own. It wasn't easy to write, it wasn't even necessarily fun, and the last stage in particular was a jungle swamp of Resistance. But I had such a pull to do it. I knew I needed to share. It was trying to emerge. Through me.

So, the question is, what are you being called to share? What ideas, what writing, what creativity will emerge if you allow it? And above all, what are you waiting for?

The time is now.

Notes

1. You can read more about To Me/By Me/Through Me/As Me in Dethmer's and his co-authors' book, The 15 Commitments of Conscious Leadership. References to these ideas crop up elsewhere in this book and my work because they, and particularly the idea of opening to 'life happening through me', have been so fundamental in this practice and in my work developing.

2. How I Became A Full-Time Coach Less Than Two Years After Starting My Training: https://www.thecoachsjourney.com/writing/how-i-became-a-full-time-coach-less-than-two-years-after-starting-my-training

Chapter Seven

Everything Starts with a Decision. So, Decide

Written on 4th August, 2017

It always, always starts with a decision. *Everything* we do starts with a decision. I've been reading a lot of Steven Pressfield recently. He talks about how, in order to beat 'Resistance' and achieve our dreams, to follow our calling, we need to 'turn pro'. How do we turn pro? Well, it starts by deciding to do it.

My friend Mike Toller told me a story about how someone was asked, 'How do you stay married for so long?'

The answer?

'Well, for a start you decide to.'

I've written before about how a lack of hope comes from a lack of freedom, and that by opening the door to the sense of possibilities, of freedom, of agency, somehow people's hope returns... And then anything can happen.

One of the reasons that coaching is powerful is essentially that your coach will ask you questions and expect answers. If you decide to answer, then you do. And when you do, then you realise that it's in your power to decide. To make a decision. To make a choice. If you come to the end of the session, then usually there will be a path forward and *you* will have decided it.

And then you see: *you can choose to change things*.

Of course, after that, you have to decide to follow that plan. Decide to keep your word. Decide to create change. You may have to decide more than once. You may have to decide every day. But it's your choice: *you decide*.

And I'm not being flippant here, I really believe it does all start with a decision. Everything, from the way we feel, to our route to work, is a decision. Simple. But this doesn't make it easy.

Some of these decisions are the hardest ones we will ever make. To leave a relationship. To quit a job. To tell a family member how they have hurt you. To say, 'You're right.' To say, 'I'm sorry.'

The challenge then, is to see the decision for what it is. Something we have control over. Something we can decide. To understand that we are the main character in our story. We are not pulled by the web of ages along destinies already plotted. We are not trapped in the web of history, passed down by our parents and ancestors through their own neuroses, fears and struggles.

We are not victims of the man, of the government, of the 'one per cent'. We are people. We are heroes.

We are the ones who say, in the face of our darkest times: I decide to move forward. I decide to change my life. I decide

I will be happy one day. I decide I will be happy today.

We are the ones who decide our children will have it better than us and work like demons to make it happen.

We are the ones who decide to love, not criticise, when the cowards in the crowd do otherwise.

We are the leaders, in our selves and in our lives.

We are the ones who cry when we feel sad. Who laugh when we feel joy. Who love when we feel love.

We are human.

We decide.

Part Two: HOW TO START

Ah, but what do I start? Where do I start? How do I start? What about all these reasons I have *not* to start?

The possibilities available to us are endless and we have to decide between them.

The demands on our time are many and we can't do or start everything.

Part Two is my offering to you for when the questions you're asking yourself are hardest and you feel you need answers.

It contains a set of ideas, thoughts, reflections, stories and practices – each of which I believe could, in some way, open up possibilities for how you can start.

Each or any of them could be the spark you need, could hold the key to getting moving. Maybe one of them shows you the thing that is stopping you and allows you to move past it. Maybe one of them shows you the way to shift your mindset, so you can see the route through the fog to the start line and beyond.

Read them looking for the one sentence or idea that will be what *you* need to break the deadlock, to grease the wheels, to get moving.

It's important that you start.

Here is what I have learned about how to do that.

Chapter Eight

The Power of a Commitment

Written on 10th August, 2017

Here's my writing practice:

Get on the train. Write for 12 minutes. Proofread once. Publish.

But it starts with a commitment. On the surface, the commitment is to post one article per week, written on the train between Waterloo and Clapham Junction.

On a deeper level, it's a commitment to beating Resistance[3] and getting more of me and my art out into the world. And underneath *that* is a commitment to finding a way for my Higher Self to express itself.

Although, I couldn't have told you all that when it started. All I could have told you is that I needed a series of tricks to get me out of my head, and stop me from getting in my own way – getting in the way of creating, of sharing any part of myself with the world.

Those tricks started with a commitment, and continued by committing to that, deciding to commit to it, every week, every day.

Sometimes it works better than others. It allows me to say more than I thought I knew. This happened last time I wrote. I didn't really know what I was going to write about, beyond an instinct that there was something important about making decisions.

But something came out that I was really proud of; which people have responded to. So, my commitment is renewed. This is going to be tough in August. I won't be on the same train because they're doing some 'improvements' at Waterloo. The practice will have to evolve. And that's risky.

Resistance can't cope with the kind of discipline, commitment and routine that make up the train writing practice. But it thrives on the times when we waver.

The diets given up after birthdays, the exercise regimes stopped after injury or holiday. So, here's another accident that I didn't mean to write about: I have to commit *now* – now that I've realised what could happen here. I have to tie myself to another month of writing at the very least. I'll write one post a week through August. They might be longer than 12 minutes, because they won't be on the same journey. But they'll be there.

If I don't commit, they won't happen.

What will you commit to this month?

What will you create?

And how will you share it?

Because as Seth Godin says, 'It's not art until you ship it.'

Notes

3. You'll have noticed several references to Steven Pressfield's 'Resistance' already in this book. As a concept – the universal force that keeps us from creating – it has been fundamental to my personal growth and creativity. You can read more in The War of Art or many of his other books.

Chapter Nine

The Only Thing Stopping You is You

Written on 27th September, 2018

I shared a video with my dad, recently. It was of coach and author Rich Litvin, sharing clearly and efficiently the experience he had learned over many years about how to talk to someone about his work as a coach.

One of the things my dad shared in response was that when he was working as a therapist in the '80s and early '90s, this kind of information just wasn't available to him. Perhaps this is because there hadn't been the thought done on this, but more, I think, because the mechanism for recording and sharing experience in this way simply wasn't available.

Now, at our fingertips, are instructional videos about almost anything you can imagine. You can take courses for free, online, on almost any subject. Books are becoming more detailed and more specialised.

And books are becoming easier to publish, which means more people can create and share them. This pattern – everything becoming easier to create and easier to share – means things that were impossible or incredibly difficult to learn are now available to anyone with a mobile phone or computer. Which, in the UK, is pretty much everyone.

Count this blessing.

It's important. Notice it. Be grateful for it. You can learn… to coach, to code, to run a business.

It's important because of this:

The availability of cheap technology, and incredibly plentiful information and communication, means that now, *the only thing stopping you is you.*

It may be your excuses around not having the time. It may be that you are prioritising other things right now. It may be that you are scared. It may be that you aren't confident and are waiting until you are. Or you aren't ready and you're waiting until the day you finally are.

But all these things are *you*. That is what is stopping you now. Just you. Only you.

That doesn't mean it's easy to solve. But it is simple.

You get to choose each of these things. How you deal with time, priorities, fear, confidence, 'readiness'.

You might not be able to see how it's you that's the blockage, but it is.

You might think that you don't know where to look, but you have Google. You can ask the questions. You can find the person who knows and ask them.

You might think that it'll take too long, or it's too late, but that's just *your* choice. And remember that humans usually underestimate what they can do in five years.

It's easier to have an excuse. Because having ultimate responsibility for what happens in life is scary. And it's tough. Because it's all on you. But here's the thing: it's where the power lies. And the control. And the freedom.

The freedom to start, because you want to. Or the freedom to not start, because you don't want to. And *only* because of that.

The freedom is yours if you want it.

Chapter Ten
The One-Line Business Plan

Written on 23rd January, 2018

Rich Litvin ran his (very successful) business for around a decade with a one-line business plan:

Meet fun and interesting people.

I tell this story to clients sometimes. It's always greeted with a smile and usually it's a smile of relief. Perhaps the relief of, 'Oh, it can be that simple.' It has opened up some wonderful clarity for people. One client, struggling with career decisions, settled on a one-line career plan. It was something like,

Do what makes the greatest positive difference.

How powerful.

When that client sits in indecision now, unsure what to do or where to start, they can check in: what here will make *the greatest positive difference?*

Speaking to Rich two weeks ago, he retold this story to me and my fellow members of the Prosperous Coach Salon, where we work together. And it's interesting how, even though I'd heard it before, it opened something new for me.

I'd been stuck in indecision. My energy was low. I was anxious. I was grumpy. I was tired. Now this may have been the upshot of coming back to work after three weeks off for Christmas. That's what I thought it was. Until Rich told the story.

As I reflected on it, I spoke about how I'd run my business. About the underlying principle that had taken me from career indecision to being a full-time coach. It came (in a perhaps not very obvious way) from a brilliant article by Richard Alderson of Careershifters and I had continued to use it for several years. Essentially, my one-line career change plan, and later my one-line business plan, was:

Follow the feeling.

Now, mine isn't quite as good a one-line business plan as Rich's, or the client I mention above, because it requires some explanation.

The *feeling*, for me, is a flicker of excitement. An instinct. It's usually located in my chest, above and in front of my heart. When faced with a decision I think, *where is the feeling greater?* Then I take a step forward down that line. Then, when faced with another decision: *where is the feeling greater?* Then I take another step.

When the feeling goes – disappears – I stop, take stock. Then think, *Now, in this decision, where is the feeling greater?* Sometimes it involves a step back, or two, or three, or many, to find where the feeling is greater. Sometimes something new opens up.

As I shared a brief version of this story with Rich, he said, 'It sounds like you have a compass.' And I do.

As I have learnt more and done more reflection, I have learnt another frame for this. This feeling happens more and more the closer I get to the *Through Me* experience. When, instead of reacting to the world (*Life Happening To Me*), and instead of creating the world I want (*Life Created By Me*), I am allowing the world to happen through me. This is the closest, so far, that I can get to fulfilling my potential, to doing my best work, to being in my zone of genius.

Rich is a listener, so he caught that, stopped and said:

'Okay, that's the challenge. The commitment for this year is to ask yourself, "What does the compass say?" and then, "What outcome here would be the world happening through me?"'

The next day, my diary was quite clear, so I sat and thought. *Where is the feeling?* And further, *where is the world happening through me?*

In particular, I sat with a decision I'd been making. Should I run a programme for coaches? My Resistance to this was great and complex:

I don't want to be typecast as someone who only works with coaches...

What if I fail?

Who am I to do this?

But the compass said *start*.

So I did.

And I learnt quite quickly whether it was the right thing to do. Just a few hours later, having put a web page live and emailed the people who had taken part in two test calls late last year, I walked along the street to meet my fiancée Emma. And the energy was flowing. I was almost lifted off my feet.

Follow the feeling.

Three people I know have described the feeling of doing their greatest work as having hands on their lower back, pushing them and supporting them. For me, it's like there's a thread in my chest, pulling me forward. So, I knew I'd taken the right step. And I've been pulled along for 10 days since then, too. That's what it's like when life is happening through me.

My world feels unlocked. My worries – about The Coach's Journey group programme, about how to price my coaching, about taking leadership in different areas – are suddenly less. I can just check in and *follow the feeling*.

What is your one-line business plan?

And where does the feeling take *you* now?

Chapter Eleven

How Do I Let My Ambition Out?

Written on 13th October, 2016

One of my coaching clients recently told me that in Spanish, the word 'ambition' has very negative connotations. In some ways I found that a relief. I had wondered if the suspicion surrounding ambition was specific to the UK, or even just to parts of the British middle classes. To see it opened, perhaps as a more significant part of the human condition, made me curious.

What is it that makes people – like me, and my client – almost nervous to talk about their ambitions?

First, perhaps, is its association with greed. There is an implicit feeling that the only people who are ambitious are greedy. For more money, for more fame. Or just for *more*.

Second, perhaps, comes the fear of failure.

I can't talk about my ambitions, because I've had dreams before and the pain of them failing is too great to let it be public by speaking of my ambition.

Or worse still,

The pain is too great to even have dreams anymore.

And third comes some sense of getting beyond one's station. In some ways this is the most dangerous, because it has the least truth to it.

'That'll never work,' your friend might say.

'Why don't you find something safer to do?' your parent might offer.

'Who am I to do this?' you might ask yourself.

The doubt and the desire for safety – for ourselves and those we love – feel important. They feel like real fear. But in the modern world, they almost always aren't.

So, the question becomes, how do I let my ambition out? How do I acknowledge and trust it?

First, speak it.

To yourself, if you need to, but ideally tell someone else.

What do you *really* want?

Chapter Twelve

Develop Your Sense of Possibility

Written on 28th July, 2017

Human beings overestimate what they can achieve in a day, a week, or even a month or a year. This is why our to-do lists so often don't get finished and always get rolled on.

And, don't forget, we grossly underestimate what we can achieve in a number of years. This is why we don't start the big projects. We don't realise how far away we'll be from where we are now in two or three years, let alone ten years if we put our minds to it. We can't grasp such a long period of time, can't feel how different we might be, how much we might be able to change ourselves and the world, so we don't start.

Once you have developed your sense of possibility enough, and understand this truth, then suddenly anything becomes possible if you reframe the time period.

Maybe you can't change career and make the same money this year, but give yourself two years, or five, or ten, and why shouldn't you? In ten years you could complete a bachelor's degree, a masters and a PhD. You could be a PhD level expert in anything! Or, in even less time, you could be fluent in any language. Well, there's possibility there.

But there's more to it than that. One of my favourite questions to ask coaching clients is,

'What would make this conversation extraordinary?'

Sometimes even,

'What would have to happen in this conversation to make it the most extraordinary conversation of your year?'

And here's the thing: not every time, but far more often than you would think, that extraordinary thing then happens. If people have the 'possibility muscle' even to answer that question – which is not always an easy thing to do – they often choose something that two people dancing with possibility and awareness and creativity can achieve in 60 or 90 minutes. Extraordinary is, it turns out, possible.

I sat down with a client recently to review our objectives. I had asked her a version of the extraordinary question before we started: 'What are the "impossible goals" for the next four months of our work together?' After only three months, we had achieved all three of the 'impossible goals'.

Part of what these questions do is move people out of the very sensible, very realistic space they are so used to spending their time in. And once you are in the space of *possibility*, you find that your mind has been playing tricks on you. More is possible than you think.

And don't forget Seth Godin's *Icarus Deception*. It's dangerous to fly too high, yes, but we never hear the other part of Daedalus' warning: it's also dangerous to fly too low.

So, come fly with me into possibility. What would have to happen to make this next hour extraordinary? What is your impossible goal for this year?

And what's the smallest, tiniest step you can take towards that extraordinary outcome?

What's the smallest, tiniest step you can take towards that impossible goal?

Chapter Thirteen
Make Impeccable Commitments to Yourself and Others

Written on 10th March, 2017

This morning, as I woke up, I had a flash of what to write about today. It was about that feeling of the light at the end of the tunnel, as you finally realise you are recovering from illness, or you first notice the start of spring.

But by the time I got on the train, my chest was tight and the feeling was far more one of frustration. Annoyance and worry had wormed their way in.

And I think, in many ways, that light at the end of the tunnel, that hope, is one side of a coin. And frustration is the other. And the coin is agency: control over your own life, control over your own destiny.

Hope comes from agency. It comes from the feeling of possibility. *You can make things happen.*

And frustration comes from agency, or lack of it. From not being able to make things happen.

Today, my frustration is about a project I'm working on, and is mixed with a sense of righteousness about what has gone wrong. *I* knew better than this. If people had listened to *me*, we wouldn't be in this mess.

Can you see how even that comes from a lack of control and agency?

Because I did know better, but I didn't manage to communicate it. I didn't control the situation. Somehow, through my own thoughts and my perception of the actions of others, I knew what I thought was right, but didn't or couldn't make it happen.

Watch for frustration: when you feel it, where have you given away your sense of agency?

In the midst of my frustration, I remembered Fred Kofman's book, *Conscious Business*, in which he talks about *impeccable coordination*. One of the fundamental parts of this is to make commitments that are impeccable: where there are no grey areas. Everyone knows whose responsibility is what. Once you've read the chapter about this kind of commitment, it becomes apparent how often in everyday life there are grey areas in our commitments.

It is in these grey areas that we release a great deal of our control. And we release our agency. We do this through blame, through huffing and gossiping about someone else. Someone who *hasn't done* something or *has done* something that has caused all sorts of trouble for us. But really, this has all happened because we allowed a shade of grey in our commitment to each other.

What if, instead, we took control? What if we used our power over our own lives to help take the grey areas out of these commitments? It isn't easy. People, me included, don't want to be held to things, because in making an impeccable commitment we open ourselves to the possibility of failure. And that fear of failure is powerful. The grey area is safety.

But through these commitments leads the path to stronger relationships. To better work. To happiness and hope and possibility. Because within the commitment is the acknowledgement that *we can do this*. And when we think we can do it, when we believe we can do it, then everything changes.

So, make impeccable, clear, black and white commitments. To others, yes, but also to yourself.

Then there is the light at the end of the tunnel. Then there is possibility.

Chapter Fourteen
The Northwest of England Way to Make Decisions

Written on 17th July, 2019

I'm part of a WhatsApp group with seven of my oldest friends. It is one of those times when technology has completely enhanced relationships: I get to speak almost every day with people who I have known for more of my life than I haven't, but who are scattered across the country. As you can imagine, for a group of 30-something men raised in the northwest of England, this involves running jokes, nicknames and a lot of talking about football.

More recently, we have developed a frame for looking at the world. It *may* have originated from my habit of giving balanced answers to questions, which my friends wanted to curtail for comedy purposes. I can't quite remember, but either way, in the group we now view the world through the frame of:

Good or Shite?

There is no in-between. There is no grey. Things are either good or they are shite.

Therefore, £4.75 is good value for a pint, but £4.76 is shite. Similarly, Harry Maguire must be a good signing for

Manchester United because he is not shite. And if someone's evening definitely hasn't been good, then it must, in fact, have been shite.

The interesting thing about this frame is that I've come across it before. In fact, I use it with clients quite often. My former coach, Rich Litvin, talks about it. Things are either, 'Hell Yes' or they are 'Hell No'. Rich *does* have a name for the in-between. In between 'Hell Yes' and 'Hell No' is just... *Hell*.

Once you play with this kind of frame in your life, you see things more clearly.

One of my clients realised that she wasn't ready to say, 'Hell No' to her business, and instead might need to say, 'Hell Yes'. It was being trapped in the hell in between that was draining her energy and thinking. *And* holding her back in her business.

Now, I'm the sort of person who is interested in specificity around language, and some of you who are reading may notice there is a subtle difference between Rich's frame and the one my friends and I play with. If you really want to prioritise in your life, then it helps if the 'yes' part of the dichotomy is a big yes. A *Hell Yes!* Because we know what a 'Hell Yes' feels like. We can check: am I 'Hell Yes!' for this or not?

That's what gets us out of doing things that we should really say 'No' to. And most of us should say 'No' more to mediocrity (or even the 'good'), socially and professionally, in order to be able to say 'Yes' to the extraordinary.

So, perhaps the true northwest of England equivalent to 'Hell Yes' or 'Hell No' is in fact 'Bloody Good' or 'Shite'.

Whether you prefer the Croydon/California version shared by Rich Litvin, or the northwest of England version shared by me and my friends, take these frames into your life. Where are you putting up with something mediocre because you simply haven't asked yourself if something is what you *really want*? And what would life look like if you played through the frame of Hell Yes or Hell No; of Bloody Good or Shite?

Try it, just for a day or a week. See your decision-making and commitments through these frames. Sometimes it is ideas like this that create space for magic to happen.

Chapter Fifteen

Take the Risk to Create the Partnerships You Need

Written on 27th January, 2017

Partnerships start with a connection. But we have lots of connections every day: with people, with organisations… and not all connections become partnerships that change our lives.

Partnerships truly start with vulnerability. They start with reaching out, exposing yourself to the possibility of rejection, offering some of yourself for nothing.

At some point, someone has to reach out. This can be hard, but there's really no other way about it. And there's a lot of fear involved. Of rejection, of being laughed at. And a lot of 'who am I to partner with this person?' Also a lot of 'why would this person want to partner with me?'

After the reaching out, if a partnership is to be created, someone else has to say, 'I want more of this.' Whether that is to another business, a potential mentor, a potential business partner or a potential lover.

But the reaching out, the risking of exposure, can be so powerful. And, as with so many things that create fear or tension in us, we can make it a practice in itself. A practice of love and of admiration and of generosity.

I learnt this from Natasha Stanley on the Careershifters blog. If you reach out to someone and say, 'I'm really inspired by what you do. I'd love to buy you a coffee and ask you about it,' then most of the time, if people can, they will. And you can double the amount of times people will do this by telling them *why* you're inspired by what they do:

'Your work is exactly what I'd like to be doing in ten years. I love the way you're changing the world.'

Imagine if someone said that to you.

Wouldn't you want to meet them?

Chapter Sixteen

Our Ingenuity is Holding Us Back

Written on 6th November, 2017

The human mind is ingenious. Completely ingenious. As ingeniously creative as it is – and let us not forget we live in an age of wonders, the likes of which almost no one 40 years ago, let alone 400 years ago, could have possibly imagined – it is also ingenious at stopping us from doing things.

I delivered a workshop on Steven Pressfield's Resistance a few months ago, and told some stories about just how ingenious we can be at stopping ourselves from doing things. How I once convinced myself that by not making a website that had been in my mind for several years, I was protecting the idea from being done by someone else, when in reality the other similar ideas I had played with *had* been done by someone else first because I *hadn't* put them out into the world.

I explained how my client, Molly Benjamin, was resisting writing an ebook, so much that she went so far as to do *other* things which she had been avoiding for years. They were done, which was fantastic, but the book remained inside her. I spoke about how, just as my dad, Pete Armstrong, was getting *really excited* about publishing his writing, which he has come back to every 10 years or so throughout his life, he got really quite ill and stopped.

Thankfully, I got the website up, Molly has launched her business (although the ebook is still to come) and my dad is back writing again, publishing his latest book just a few weeks ago.

But there's another element I want to turn my focus to today. It isn't just 'not getting things done' that we are ingenious at. We are also sometimes ingenious at not being happy.

Gay Hendricks, in his book *The Big Leap*, talks about the Upper Limit Problem. He describes how, because of narratives and stories we tell ourselves, usually starting in childhood, almost all of us have an Upper Limit Problem. This means that, as we reach the maximum level of happiness that our narrative says we are allowed to have, we find a way to avoid exceeding that limit. We sabotage ourselves. We get ill. We procrastinate. We engage in unhelpful or unhealthy behaviour. And we worry, so, so much.

I am currently on the other side of the world from my native UK and, apart from the desire for a sprawling house in England near my family and friends and a couple of other little things like really nice pyjamas, I am living the life I set out in a vision document for what my day would look like in five years, if everything turned out remarkably.

The universe opened this up for me less than six months after I wrote that vision. And yet, I spent the first few days here fighting with myself, worrying furiously about everything from the internet, to getting a £100 refund on some insurance, to whether I was wasting my time not working enough, to whether I was wasting my time working too much. And, yes, there was jetlag. And, yes, it is hard to move countries. But above all, there was my Upper Limit Problem.

So, the question is, where in your life is your Upper Limit Problem showing up?

Where are you stopping yourself from finding happiness, not because you can't have it, but because of some out-of-date story, no longer factually accurate or useful, which tells you that for some reason you shouldn't have more happiness because you aren't worthy, or you'll outshine others, or some other nonsense.

Because you can have it, if you want it.

And you are worthy. I promise.

Chapter Seventeen

Release the Pressure of the Victim

Written on 10th February, 2017

Ah, the feeling of release from pressure. There's nothing like it! A feeling that things are back in your control, that there is momentum. Often, that is the difference between feeling happy about our lives and the mounting frustration or deathly emptiness at the other end of the spectrum.

Clients have spoken to me about it ('If I could just do something so there was a sense of possibility...') and I've also nudged them towards it, coaching them to take the small steps that show them just how in control of their lives they are.

I've done it myself. Shifting from the idea that I'm the victim, that I'm waiting for something, and that the moment I'm looking for is beyond my control – to the realisation that I'm *choosing* to wait.

At that point comes the first release. And at the point where I later take control, that's when things really open up.

Why is this so important? Why does taking a small step, having a sense of hope, a sense of possibility, make such a difference in our lives?

Well, I think we all have a deep desire – an evolutionary one – to be in control. To be free to choose. To be free.

It's this that leads to the desire for democratic control. But in our personal lives, the sad thing is that most of the time we are tricking ourselves. We have *so much* control over our lives. Especially those of us fortunate enough to have been born into a democracy: we have more freedom, more control and more agency than any people in the history of the world. More than princes and kings.

I have to say, it is an enormous pleasure and privilege that in my work I get to see people realise that. It's a magical moment.

Where are you not stepping forward into your sense of control?

Chapter Eighteen

Create Space for Magical Thinking

Written on 30ᵗʰ September, 2016

I had a realisation a few days ago, that sometimes magic happens when you think about things for longer than you think you should think about them.

I was thinking about the magic of the shift from the limitations of fixed, pessimistic, 'can't do', sceptical thinking, into the excitement and buzz of 'can do' possibility-thinking.

I'm sure you've been past that point before. It's something that happens about three drinks into an evening with friends, where you relax enough to talk about some of the things that are really important to you, and no one stops you because everyone else is in that space too.

This isn't about dwelling on the problems longer; it's a different type of thinking. It's the excitement of idea generation, of optimism about forming these ideas, and of the possibility that they could happen. And if they did, everything might change.

Coaching is a great space for this, because a coach will slow you down when you try to skate over things, ask you questions about the things you mention and may even simply invite you to 'tell me some more about that'. What a rare invitation that is, leading you to think about something for longer than you normally would, creating space for what seems like magic to happen.

And I can tell you from my experience as a coach and a client that this can, indeed, lead to magical moments of realisation.

We (the world) are really good at the first, sceptical type of thinking, especially around the things that are really important to us. It's a safety mechanism to keep us safe from being vulnerable, being 'out there', being disappointed.

But when we create more of the excitement of the second type of thinking, then things are different. Because it leads to great things, magical things, and who doesn't need more magic in their lives.

Chapter Nineteen
The Knottiness of Change

Written on 31ˢᵗ March, 2017

This week, my head felt full. It felt like all the thoughts inside it were tangled in knots as I tried to think through the change I'm facing in my life this week, as I leave my part-time role at Clore Leadership Programme and take my coaching work full time.

One of the things I've been saying to people is that this requires a shift in identity for me. I now have to accept that part of my identity is that I can start a business and make it work. And this isn't something I had even considered a few years ago. And, of course, there are other shifts in who I am as I move into this next phase.

And then I thought of some of the other shifts of identity I have had over the years.

And in each of those there was confusion and sometimes real pain. There was this knottiness that left me tired and frustrated.

Of course, if you are changing the way you see yourself, if you are changing the things you do, the viewpoints and places from which you make decisions and decide your future, then that's going to be hard. You can't fall back on all your habits from before.

I once heard Tim Ferriss say something like, 'If I always did what I was qualified to do, I would be pushing a broom somewhere.'

To do something we are under-qualified for, to change our identity to something new, we have to go to a new level. We have to learn how to be that person and learning requires us to stretch ourselves beyond what we know already.

And that can feel knotty.

But that doesn't mean we shouldn't do it.

Chapter Twenty
Make a Bet on Future You

Written on 20ᵗʰ April, 2018

I'm in Los Angeles for a coaching event. Santa Monica, to be precise. In the airport, before I set off, I posted on Facebook that 95 per cent of the reason for me coming was to look glamorous and successful. Of course, I was joking, but it is cool, right? It is to me, at least. I've flown out to LA to meet my coach. To learn. To develop myself. That is cool.

I was reflecting today on the reality of this trip. And one part of the reality is that, to be able to afford to make it at this moment in time, I needed to borrow money from my fiancée and my mum.

I am very grateful to them for allowing me to spend against my future earnings now. Because that's what I'm doing really: I'm betting on Future Me.

I'm betting that this event will help me generate income, one way or another, greater than what it costs me. In some ways... In other ways, I'm saying there are very few things I can spend money on that are more important than developing myself, through experiences and learning.

But it's a good business decision too. For those of us who want to create more of what we want in the future, whatever that may be, investing in ourselves is a good decision. For those of us who have the power to generate extra income for ourselves, or for whom our business depends almost solely on us, if you ask me it's a no-brainer.

Sometimes I still need to talk myself – the me that worked in charities for years, squeezing every penny out of the organisations' incomes, and every bit of value from the often-small salaries that I earned. I still need to talk myself into investing in me and my business. How many extra clients would I have to get to make this investment pay for itself? In that frame, the investment and the loans look incredibly sensible.

And that got me thinking about all the other ways I've found the money to do the things I want to do. The things that were calling me.

For years, I worked on a small salary in the arts, spending my savings and my energy to do work that I thought was important, and which I wanted to do. I scrimped and saved, on everything from my lunch to what I did in my spare time.

In my coaching business, I've borrowed money from my parents and Emma on several occasions.

I've negotiated discounts on training and payment plans for coaching.

I've taken advantage of free and discounted workshops and classes.

I've eaten out less, said no to things, not been on holiday, not been out, taken my own lunch and many other little things, in order to get resourceful and make things happen.

I've worked jobs I didn't really like, and coached in the evenings and at weekends, waking up tired just to do it all again.

To pay for my coach training, I spent using an interest free credit card for almost the whole fee, and paid it back over something like 18 months.

It's important for me to share this because *there is a way*. There is a way to make happen what you want to happen. To be resourceful. To create what you want. But you have to believe.

And you have to take action. And you have to ask for help.

Chapter Twenty-One

The Four Steps for Getting Into Action

Written on 19th October, 2018

I finished reading a book today. That's not that unusual. I'm a reasonably prolific reader, working my way through a number of books each year. The difference about this one is that it took me almost six months to read, even though I read it regularly, every week and most working days.

Earlier this year, I couldn't find a way to make myself read non-fiction. I just never felt like it. But learning by reading non-fiction is a part of how I develop myself as a coach (someone once joked 'your coach is someone who reads books so you don't have to'). And I wanted to read non-fiction, but I just *couldn't*. In the times when I normally read (lunchtimes and before bed) I always felt like I needed to read fiction, switching off in a way that (for me) a great novel can help me do.

In the end, here's how I managed to get back into reading non-fiction: I decided I would read for 15 minutes (roughly the amount of time it takes to drink my morning coffee) each morning when I am working at home. I would do this every time, as I drank my coffee. Thus, my worries about reading non-fiction dissipated.

Some days I would read *so little*. Maybe a couple of paragraphs, read over and over again as my mind flew everywhere else but the book. This was *not* effective reading. But it was reading. Every day. And I kept doing it. I kept making progress. And I got loads from reading the book. An article inspired by it, which I posted a couple of weeks ago, has now been read over 2,000 times in a fortnight.

I didn't always manage to read. Sometimes I forgot. But when I did that, I didn't give up. I recommitted.

That is essentially the same pattern, the same practice, that led to this post being written. I'm thinking of putting together a book of these 12-minute pieces, partly to showcase my work and collect it all into one place, and partly to say: Look! You can write a book. And all you need is 12 minutes per week, the commitment to sit down and do it, and the choice to recommit when you slip.

That got me thinking about what it is that stops others from taking action. People who know what they want – or at least they say they do – but still don't take action. What I'm about to outline is simple, but not easy. Here is some/most/all of what I've learned about how to get into action and create things:

1. Decide on the habit

Everything starts with a decision. Schedule it and sit down. No matter what. If you want to write, schedule when you will do it, then sit down when the time comes. If you want to invite people into a coaching conversation with you, schedule when you will do it and sit down when the time comes. If you want to do exercise in the morning, schedule when you will do it and sit down (or stand up, or run) when the time comes. Easier said than done, but this is *fundamental*. If you don't create the time for whatever you want, then you can never get it. And time is yours to create: you can choose how you spend that time, and each time you say 'Yes' to a coffee in your writing time, or say 'Yes' to a lie-in during your exercise time, you are saying 'No' to whatever you had chosen. You can choose, so choose.

2. When you miss the chance, don't beat yourself up

Don't think, *Ah, I'm just someone who can't do X*. Just ask yourself: 'Do I want to do this?' If the answer is yes, then ask: 'Am I willing to recommit to my schedule?' Then recommit, and next time it comes, sit down. If you don't manage that time, either, then ask yourself the questions again. Then recommit, and sit down.

3. Things are never ready

So, don't wait for it. Perfectionism is Resistance, and the sure-fire way to beat it is to share before you are ready. Send before you are ready, publish before you are ready. 100 per cent ready is always too much. 80 per cent ready is usually too much. 20 per cent – if you trust the Pareto principle – is probably about right. Share when you don't think it's ready.

4. Confidence is a myth

Of course, it's not actually a myth, it's a thing. I know that. What is a myth is that you need to have it before you do something. I once wrote about confidence: it's actually just the embodied knowledge that if you take action you can get closer to what you want. Rich Litvin put it more snappily: confidence is a result, not a requirement. When you take action, when you speak up, when you share your work, when you work out, then AND ONLY THEN, will you become confident.

Everyone doubts themselves – or at least they do if they are doing anything that truly matters. EVERYONE. The game then, is to act in spite of the doubt. And these four steps, these are how I do it.

Part Three: WHY START?

Creativity is hard. This book wouldn't be here if it wasn't.

I wouldn't have needed to accidentally write it and you wouldn't have ended up reading it. And sometimes, at least for me, a question arises:

Why even bother?

And the answer is that creativity is important. It matters. At its deepest level, creativity is making something from nothing; bringing into the world something that didn't exist before. That's how things change. That's almost the only way things change. That's why the world needs each and all of us to step up and create. Create change, create art, create a better world together.

But creativity is also important to each of us.

Creativity, the sense that we can make something from nothing, is what empowers us and excites us. It's what shifts us from feeling like a victim of circumstance to seeing that we have the power to choose in our lives; the ability to be the main character in our story. That inspiration is available to any and all of us. And once you have become someone who creates, life is different.

For each of us, the reason that makes fighting the battle with our Resistance and running the gauntlet of making something will be different. But it matters. Creativity tilts us, as individuals and as a world, towards heaven and away from hell. So please, fight that battle and run that gauntlet. It matters. It's worth it.

In Part Three, you'll find out why I believe that, with my heart and my soul.

Chapter Twenty-Two
Death Changes Everything

Written on 22nd April, 2019

Death changes things. In fact, it changes everything.

I read a quote recently, which said something like this:

'Like dying, erring is something that we acknowledge definitely happens to everyone, while simultaneously ignoring the fact that it therefore will definitely happen to us.'

It's far harder to ignore the fact of erring when your error – or that of someone close to you – has significant and seriously damaging effects on people around you. And it's harder to ignore the fact of your future death when someone you know dies.

Death is one of life's few certainties. There's very little we can do about it and we don't necessarily know when it comes. Many people find themselves ignoring these facts, believing somehow that this makes life more enjoyable. That remembering or thinking about death – ours, or that of those we love – will make life worse. My experience, and the experience of those I've worked with, is exactly the opposite.

I've written elsewhere about the power of considering your death. In the words of the Zen saying, of 'dying before you die, so that you can truly live'. And since I wrote about that, I have regularly invited clients to consider their death: to consider what would have happened if, at their death, life had worked out extraordinarily.

Or, conversely, to consider what would make them sad if, at the end of their life, it either had or had not happened. Each time I have taken clients to the place where they consider their own mortality, I have seen powerful results. In fact, I would say nothing has had as profound or as quick an impact on people's lives; on everything from their relationships, to their family, to their time management and prioritisation.

The fragility of life is important to remember, however you remember it.

It will remind you of the things that really matter to you deep down. The relationships that are important, the material things that matter and those that don't, the fears that hold you back that you wish didn't.

It releases you from the strangling grip of your ego, desperate to protect your sense of identity. It releases you from the dreams of the past, the 'shoulds' and 'if-onlys' that stop you taking action.

It reminds you that the second-best time to start is *now*.

It reminds you that, deep down, you *do* care about things, and you *do* want to create something wonderful in your life, whatever wonderful means to you.

It reminds you that you – *yes, you* – have your own definition of success, which matters to *you*, the deeper version of you that exists inside. You can use that one (not one you inherited from someone else) to be the guiding star in your life, the true north, the compass that you follow as you make decisions and change things and say 'Yes' and say 'No'.

These are the powers of facing your mortality. Of sitting down and writing the eulogy you would love to be given at the end of your life. Of making the list of things which, at the end of your life, would make you sad, and turning them into a commitment to live by a sense of *I will not let that be the legacy of my life*.

And, really, what is the other choice? The other choice is just to sleepwalk through life. To hope that one day you will wake up and things will have turned out well. To let fear of a certainty – one you can do nothing about – hold you back.

Some people worry that if they face their own mortality then there will be nothing left to live for, and life will descend into panic or a not-caring-about-anything nihilism. But that's not what I've seen. What I've seen is people stepping up in their lives, and being the heroes that deep down they really are.

Chapter Twenty-Three
The Power of Creativity

Written on 25th August, 2016

My first school report was a good report. This probably came as a relief, as I was nine years old and my family and I really had no idea how this school thing was going to go (I was home-educated until that point, a story for another time). The report wasn't perfect, but in all but one area it came back positive.

The exception was art. In my art report, Mrs Ramsay – a great teacher and a woman who had a real effect on me and is now sadly missed – wrote something that included the devastating few words, '...but Robbie has no real talent at art.'

This story has a good arc, because only a few months later I won a regional painting competition entered by all the 8-10-year-olds in the local primary schools and had my painting turned into a postcard that you can still buy in Ingleton in North Yorkshire. Ha! Take that Mrs Ramsay!

Winning that competition is still one of the things in my life that I am most proud of. Part of that, perhaps, was the triumph over Mrs Ramsay's report. But at the time, I remember not being joyful about winning. The judges praised the depth I had given the pool around the swimmers, but I had just refilled my paint, making it darker in some places purely by accident. They praised the straightness of the figure by the side, but I had simply forgotten to paint his second leg. It all felt 'by chance' that it was a good painting and I suspect that my nine-year-old self didn't take joy in that, because, well, he knew he didn't have any talent.

Brené Brown says that almost everyone has a story from school about their creativity being belittled by a teacher. And they remember them clearly. I don't want you to think that I am belittling teachers; Mrs Ramsay was one of thousands of brilliant people who, every year, make an immeasurable contribution to our country and the world through the care, hard work and inspiration they provide to young people.

But creativity is a fragile thing in people. Thinking of myself as 'operational' rather than 'creative' played a significant role in the decisions I took in the first ten years of my career.

No one told me that creativity was important for more than art. No one told me it was at the root of successful business, of politics. No one told me it was how we use our ingenuity to solve the world's problems. No one told me it was important for health and wellbeing. No one told me it was about joy, accidental or otherwise, brought to ourselves and others.

Well, for the last one, maybe some people did; maybe even Mrs Ramsay, at a different time. And to them, I say thank you.

But these reasons, these are why we must create: for ourselves and for others, no matter what story we hold about how creative we are.

* * *

Note: As part of the editing process for this book, I went back to my school report from 1994 to check this quote and I found something fascinating. My memory was clear and solid that what Mrs Ramsay had said was what I wrote in this article: '...but Robbie has no real talent at art.' When I went back to the report, however, what she had written was something much less extreme: 'Robbie's artwork tends to be somewhat immature at present, but as his confidence grows, I am sure he will develop a sensitivity in this subject.'

There are two reasons I have left this in and written this rather lengthy footnote. First, because our memory is far from the reliable record we think it is. In episodes 3 and 4 of *Revisionist History Season 3*, Malcolm Gladwell explains in shocking detail just how much our storytelling brains distort what we remember of the past. Those episodes are worth checking out to learn just how good our memory is not.

Second, I wanted to leave this in because it demonstrates how sensitive we can be to criticism, perhaps particularly around creativity, as Brené Brown suggests. Even a fairly gentle criticism of my art left me with a story of 'no real talent'. So, remember, we must be so sensitive with our children. And remember, the criticism you remember may not be the criticism that actually happened.

Lastly, I'm sorry Mrs Ramsay that I have carried that story about you around with me and I'm sorry I retold it in this original way in my article. You looked after me really well at a difficult time, as you looked after many hundreds of other children. Sending love and gratitude to you, wherever you are.

Chapter Twenty-Four

Change is What Happens When Seven Billion People Try to Do Their Best

Written on 18th August, 2016

At the station where I get on my train into London, there are a load of signs that proudly proclaim it 'Britain's busiest railway station'.

As a friend of mine pointed out, this is a strange thing to advertise. 'Mmm, a really busy railway station, can't wait to go there!' said no one ever.

But it also feels true, and pretty amazing, especially when surrounded by the incredible flow of commuters into London on a weekday, who then diffuse off the station into the flow at Waterloo before slipping into the tube, the buses; the rivers of people who cross one bridge or another, to then walk down one pathway or another.

I saw a TED talk where the speaker, Robert Wright, pointed to how life has gradually become more complex and connected. From single celled organisms, through to more complex ones, to different species and ecologies. With that in mind, and on this train journey, I didn't need Wright's diagram to show the complex, connected system that the world – that life – now is. It's as clear in London's public transport as it is in a picture of the earth lit up by the connected cities and towns of the human race.

It makes me wonder, how does change happen? How can anyone or anything influence such a flow of people, such a complex, connected organism as the planet and all the people on it? Especially as each week more and more people across the world are connected even more closely by the internet.

And, of course, I don't know.

But I'm reading Brené Brown's *Rising Strong* at the moment, and there is a profound chapter about her discovering the idea of living from the assumption that everyone is doing their best.

And when thinking about how change happens, as part of this amazing and incredibly complex system, I can't help but think – in my attempt to live more from that assumption, for the generosity it promotes in me, and the judgment it removes – that change is just what happens when there are seven billion people trying to do their best.

For themselves, their families, and the world at large.

Chapter Twenty-Five
Being Someone Who Writes

Written on 8th March, 2019

It's 8:36pm on a Friday night. I know what I 'should' be doing: any number of Friday night things. But I'm not. Because I'm *someone who writes* and shares a piece of writing every week.

It's not quite true, of course. Over the last few months there have been a number of weeks where I haven't shared a piece of writing in this practice – the practice that has produced around 100 articles like this one, written in about 12 minutes – but in each of those weeks where I haven't published something, it has been because I have shared something else, something that has felt bigger and more significant. I chose not to publish.

This week, until about an hour ago, I just forgot.

At other times in my life, I would have just written this off. I would have said, 'Ah, what a shame!' But this week, mid-pint in the pub on the corner, I remembered. And as soon as I told my wife, she understood. We got back and I sat down at my desk, set the timer and started to write. And she got it, because *this is a thing I do.*

It's not easy to become *someone who writes.*

It takes work, it takes commitment, it takes recommitment when you slip. And, worst of all, it takes starting. That's the hardest bit. It's like physics. As you lean against something, pushing it, trying to move it, the first millimetre is the hardest. The second is a fraction easier, and then, a little later, the thing is moving, rolling along. Then, you are a person pushing a car or a boulder along. It's almost harder at that point *not* to be pushing it than it is to be pushing it. Even if you stop pushing for a moment, the thing keeps moving, and before you know it, you are pushing it again, keeping it in motion.

That's what the practice of becoming *someone who does something* is like. Or at least that's what it was like for me.

I'm also *someone who exercises.*

I didn't used to be. Well, that's not true. I was, then I wasn't, then I was, then I wasn't, then I was. And, now I am. But the first bit, that's the hardest bit. It's hard because it's hard (literally hard) to lift yourself off the ground or run the extra metres. It's hard because it's so easy to be *someone who doesn't exercise.* That takes no effort at all.

I spoke to a friend of mine today. She's in a new phase of her life, creating a portfolio of work that fits with the unique gifts she has. To me it seems obvious that the boulder she is pushing is already moving and soon will be moving fast (if she wants it to), but to her, the boulder is barely moving and she has no sense that once it's moving it is going to just keep rolling. And the reason it will keep rolling is because all her unique talents are coming out, being expressed in ways they weren't before. The patterns are emerging, but she doesn't know what they are yet. She doesn't know that she is going to become *someone who creates work for themselves*.

And one day, when we're already *someone who writes*, or *someone who exercises* or *someone who creates work for themselves*, we tell a simple story of how that happened. And people who look at us, they just see the end product. Ah, that's just *someone who writes*. They don't see the challenges; they don't see those first agonising moments as the boulder started to move. They don't see the blood, sweat and fears that almost stopped us pushing. They don't see the moments when we stumbled, almost lost control, and decided, just as we were about to give up, to recommit, one more time. Those are the things we *must* remember.

It's a complex story how we make ourselves into something new. How we create a new part of our identity. How we become – in the end, without thinking – *someone who parents really well*, or *someone who runs a business*, or *someone who walks 10,000 steps every day* when we didn't used to be that before.

The forces of the world seem arrayed against us. The attention-grabbing dopamine hit of our electronic devices. The mechanical pull of work, day after day. The voices in our head that tell us, perhaps based on something that used to keep us safe, to stay as we are, to not risk change.

It takes courage to change. It takes grit and determination. And then (from the outside, 'all of a sudden', but from the inside after months or years of graft and work) we are different. We are changed.

It's hard. And it's worth it.

Chapter Twenty-Six

The Magic of Small Leadership

Written on 31ˢᵗ July, 2019

The psychologist and coach Robert Holden told a story about leadership at a recent workshop I attended. He spoke about a friend of his whose leadership he deeply admired. She changed the face of her town by what I'll call *Small Leadership*. And I'll say at the outset, that I believe Small Leadership is what matters in a society far, far more than Big Leadership.

The Small Leadership that Holden's friend exhibited was demonstrated by placing a hanging basket outside her shop. This Small Leadership and the conversations it created changed things, slowly at first, and then faster and faster. Soon, the high street of the town where she lived had hanging baskets everywhere; the environment was beautiful, and more plants were planted. What amazing Small Leadership.

Holden's story reminded me of one of the ways I try to show Small Leadership.

I decided to do this after an experience several years ago. I was investigating what career path to choose and went along to several open evenings for psychotherapy courses.

I met a really great guy, Alex, at one of them. We had great conversations, but we didn't agree a way to stay connected. I felt sad afterwards. I had got on really well with Alex, and I didn't have many friends at the time who were as interested in how people work as I was. It felt like he could have been that person.

Then the universe helped me. At another psychotherapy open evening a few weeks later, *the same guy was there.* This time, we got the tube home together. But we still hadn't agreed to stay in touch. Just coming to the final stop, I realised I wasn't willing to let this opportunity go, so I said, 'I'd really like to stay in touch. Would that be okay?' or something like that. It was like asking someone out. He said, 'I'd really like that' and we swiftly swapped email addresses before one of us had to get off.

I've realised that ever since then I have been taking Small Leadership in creating connection in my life.

I have busted through my Resistance about staying connected with people. I'm now always the person who says, 'How can I stay in touch?' and collects emails or LinkedIn contacts or whatever. And I'm the person who goes online after an event and tracks down the people I had great conversations with. That might be why some of you are reading this.

I show the leadership and then I trust *them* to say, 'I'd rather not,' or ignore my email or whatever, if *they* don't want to. That's fine. I've done my bit for creating more connection in the world, just like someone who hangs a hanging basket has done their bit for creating beauty in their town.

The thing is, Small Leadership is how everything changes. Matt Ridley, in his fascinating book, *The Evolution of Everything*, makes an argument that there are *no great people*. It's similar to Malcolm Gladwell's argument in *Outliers*: there are just really good people who happen to be in the right place at the right time.

What matters then, once someone has been in the right place at the right time, is how *everyone else* responds. It's how *everyone else* shows Small Leadership. It's one thing to be, let's say, Daniel Goleman, who as I understand made popular the phrase Emotional Intelligence. But it's another thing to be one of the millions of people who saw that was an important idea and used it to create a more empathic world.

It's one thing to be Brené Brown and (as she would probably say) stumble accidentally on creating an amazing TED Talk on vulnerability. It's another to take Small Leadership in each of our lives to be more vulnerable with those around us and *change the world*.

It's one thing to create an innovation in education or business. And it's another to take Small Leadership by taking action in your life and spreading that innovation to improve people's lives.

Don't think that Big Leadership is better than Small Leadership. Taking Small Leadership in the ways that matter to you: perhaps kindness, or smiling, or love, or conversations with strangers, or aesthetics, or courage, or creativity. That is what matters.

What *you* *do* matters. In every small way you create change.

That is the magic of Small Leadership.

Chapter Twenty-Seven

Take Responsibility in Your Life

Written on 16ᵗʰ February, 2018

There is an epidemic of crippling choice in the modern world – a sense of *listlessness*.

Listlessness, despite the fact that we have more possibilities open to us than ever before. Despite the fact that more opportunities are open to more people than ever. That the world is more equal than ever, that more of us than ever have the wealth and education to make choices rather than being trapped at the whims of someone else.

Despite all this, we are a ship adrift on an ocean with no horizon in sight, as one of my clients told me when we first met.

But how can this be?

I had seen it many times with clients, but it was only when I watched a documentary about the clinical psychologist Jordan Peterson, and later heard him speak, that I began to see the answer.

Peterson speaks about *rights* and *responsibilities*. And he brought a distinction that I had never seen before. That meaning in our lives – the direction to sail our ship in – comes from responsibilities and *never* from rights.

Peterson speaks directly about this to men in particular. Because, he says, there is something particularly masculine about responsibility.

I was on a course last year, where two sessions were led by Karen Kimsey-House, a coach, author and leader who, among other things, founded CTI, one of the world's largest coach training programmes. She spoke about the importance of bringing both the Sacred Feminine *and* the Sacred Masculine into our work.

It is this I believe Peterson is speaking to when he speaks of rights and responsibilities.

Rights are a part of the Sacred Feminine. They are a sense of potential, the chance to do anything, and they are a void. A sea to be adrift in.

Responsibility is a part of the Sacred Masculine. It is a lightning bolt of drive. Responsibility brings possibility, and it demands action and direction.

And we all need some measure of each of these in our lives.

For women, where the Sacred Feminine likely makes up more of their spirit, responsibilities have disappeared, and new rights and choices have become available.

Women now have the right to choose to have a career, to choose to have a family, to choose to have children by themselves if they wish, to choose to never have them. And this choice is cause for celebration. In this choice, responsibility is gone: no longer are they constrained by the traditional responsibility to hold the family together, to look after the house.

No longer, even, do any of us feel an evolutionary responsibility to the human race to have several children to continue the development of our species. No longer do we have a responsibility to our family to continue our line. We don't think like that anymore. And while these rights should be celebrated, I have seen many women – particularly in their late 20s and 30s – sitting across from me wrestling with the choice in front of them. What is their responsibility? What is their responsibility to society, to the women who went before and fought for these rights, to their feelings, to their family, to the deepest part of their souls?

And this challenge is keen and painful for those of us whose characters – whether through gender or some other mix of factors – hold more of the Sacred Masculine. The crisis for men in the modern world is that our traditional roles have been taken away from us and we are left adrift in the void.

No longer are we needed as a provider and protector for our women and our families, for our societies. No longer are we required to fight for our values or for our country. No longer are we (in many cases) even *needed* by our communities. Indeed, many of us find that we are not part of any of the traditional communities – villages, churches – which have been a part of human culture for millennia. There is no societal message on the responsibility of a man in the modern world. Not an *active* one, not a *lightning bolt* of responsibility. There is just a vacuum: do not do these things. Okay, so then what?

What do we do now? What do we – men and women – have responsibility for, now that the old frameworks are gone, and the rights and choice which have been fought for are here?

Well, now we have to choose.

Now we have to look around ourselves and *choose* to have responsibility. Decide to take on this thing – responsibility – which will bring meaning to our lives and take the human race that bit closer to heaven or utopia.

And decide to offer responsibility to others: to bring them with you, to give them meaning, to show them they can change things.

You don't know how much difference you can make – to yourself, to your family, to your community, to the world.

And until you take responsibility, you won't find out.

Chapter Twenty-Eight

What Do We Say to the God of Death?

Written on 11th September, 2019

Ah, death.

There you are again. Circling my client, present in the life of a stranger here, everywhere, across the world.

I found myself writing something like this in an email today:

'A sense of our own mortality is a powerful tool for allowing us to understand what is deeply important in our life.'

I've written before about how author and consultant Fred Kofman says that CEOs who have had a near death experience are better leaders than those who haven't, and how Kofman guides people he works with through a controlled experience to show them their mortality.

Death, you are a constant, you are always here. You are uncomfortable and you are certain. You are something we can try to control, but we know, in the end, that we aren't able to fight you off forever. Some of my favourite stories and favourite characters deal with death.

The image that comes to my mind is of David Gemmell's ageing warrior, Druss, standing on battlements, shaking his fist at the sky, denying Death for another day.

And Arya Stark, George R.R. Martin's bolshy girl turned ruthless assassin, knows what to say to the God of Death: 'Not today.'

If that, then, is all we can do: stand and fight death defiantly; say to him or her, 'Not today'. Then what?

Then make life count.

Wake up. Don't sleepwalk through it. Do whatever it takes to wake up. Write yourself a eulogy, think about what would make you sad at the end of your life. Splash yourself in the face with icy water.

Use the tools you have available to do this: connect to something bigger by going into nature or singing with a group or connecting to a cause that matters to you.

Feel something. Today. Take yourself there. Let yourself go there.

Make life count.

Make something better. Just a little bit, if that's all you can do.

As Jordan Peterson says, if where you need to start with this is to get out of bed, well, that's better than not getting out of bed.

If creating a tiny bit of order from what feels like overwhelming chaos in your life is all you can do, well, that's better than not creating any order from the chaos.

If you can choose, in a moment, to listen less to the more base, animal parts of you, and listen more to the higher, nobler, wiser parts of you instead, then do that. Do it as often as you can. Be kinder, be more skilful, leave less mess in the wake of your relationships.

Make life count.

Heal something. Anything. Pay someone back. Make an apology. You can't guarantee that something will be healed, or will go back to how it was, but you can do your part. And that's something, eh?

Plant something. Anything. If you can, make it something amazing, like the woodland that my mum (with help from my dad, me and many others) planted nine years ago. Negotiate for the land, like she did. Ask for the trees, like she did. No one who walks through that wood won't be enhanced by it, won't be more alive, now and for many years.

Start something. Anything. But above all, don't leave it unstarted. Don't leave it untried.

Make life count.

Or, at least, try. If you've tried then that, at least, is something.

Chapter Twenty-Nine
We Don't All Get Happy Endings

Written on 10th May, 2018

I was talking to my brother the other day. We were speaking of relatives who find themselves, in the latter stages of their lives, ill and alone.

And he said, 'I realised that we don't all get happy endings.'

These words stayed with me.

This isn't about death. We all go there. It isn't about dying surrounded by our family. We can't all have that.

It's about an end to our lives, of years or even decades, trapped in our home by an inward spiral of illness and aloneness.

You may know someone like this.

And the rub is this: it happens through a series of circumstances. Yes, maybe there are certain ones among us who, by genes or chance, are more likely to end up like that. But it could happen to any of us. And some of these circumstances are within our control.

We have to believe that.

They aren't easy things, though. There are choices. Decisions we make. Life is hard. It is suffering. It hurts. We must choose, decide in the face of *hard*, in the face of *suffering*, in the face of *hurt*. We must fight a battle against life. Refuse to back down.

It is about leaning. *Always leaning.* Whenever you can. Leaning out, not in.

Towards connection, not disconnection.

Towards trust, not mistrust.

Towards kindness, not cruelty.

Towards little changes, not paralysis.

Towards love, not hurt.

Towards curiosity, not judgment.

Towards 'I don't know', not 'I'm certain'.

Towards courage, not cowardice.

Towards receiving, not just giving.

Towards giving, not just receiving.

Towards vulnerability, not false invulnerability.

Towards recommitting, not giving up.

Towards reaching out, not retreating in.

It's hard, sometimes. I know.

But we don't all get happy endings. So please. Please. Lean with me.

Chapter Thirty
Creativity, Fear and Freedom

Written on 24th March, 2017

The first time I wrote one of these pieces, I was scared. So scared.

I was scared of writing it and I was scared of publishing it. I couldn't tell you what I was scared of, but I was. My coach, Joel, nudged me into committing to publishing five, which was good, because the commitment to write five meant I couldn't give up after just one. And by the time I'd written five in the space of two weeks, I was thinking about how I would carry it on.

What started as a way to batter through my Resistance to sharing myself with the world has become a writing practice. I do it partly because Seth Godin talks powerfully about how writing his daily blog has affected his *thinking* as much as his writing. And I do it partly because people have told me how much they like the writing, and somewhat surprisingly to me, they do. My former colleague, Lesa Dryburgh, told me last week that my thoughts on partnerships made it into a talk she gave to a group she was working with. And I do it for myself, because I can see and feel the value of creating. Of something emerging from nothing, coming into the world because I create it.

And it doesn't scare me so much anymore. I still don't look forward to it. I have Resistance in the form of boredom not fear.

'Oh, God, have I got to write today? Can't I just read on the train?'

And I remind myself that, yes, I have got to write today.

But the fear has gone. At least in the way it was. I've battered through that Resistance. I've transcended the fear that stopped me even posting on Facebook about anything, let alone *creating something* and posting it online. I've levelled up. I'm someone who writes now.

But the fact that the fear is different, is less paralysing, is less altogether – that's bothering me this morning. Because if I've levelled up, the question surely is, how do I level up again?

What's next?

This is the question that has been occupying me lately, as I move towards a new stage in my life.

What's the next barrier to overcome? What is the next Resistance to battle through?

I haven't always asked these questions of myself. They are difficult questions to ask, and even more difficult to answer. But as I write this, and although I know that these are important questions to ask, I wonder if that kind of fear will ever return again.

Because, as Jo Hunter, Co-Founder and CEO of the social enterprise 64 Million Artists says, creativity is the route to agency. Once you have created something, you have been vulnerable, and you have seen what you can do. And you have seen that, whatever your fear is, the worst almost never happens.

And then you're free.

Chapter Thirty-One

Don't Let Your Resistance Beat You

Written on 18th August, 2017

Resistance is everywhere and it's devious. It's stopping us doing the things we want to do. First, it stops us in ways we're familiar with: we check Facebook, we tweet, we reply to emails, we do all manner of procrastination. Then, if we're lucky – and if we *decide* to beat that through discipline and tricks and apps to stop us checking Facebook – it stops us in other ways.

It stops us with fear and self-doubt.

No one will want to read this. No one will ever be moved by this music. It's too ordinary.

We think,

Who am I to be interviewing people? Who am I to be starting a business? Who am I to be coaching people? Who am I to be leading?

If Resistance hasn't already stopped us by procrastination, then it often stops us here.

Either way, we keep our heads down and we stay 'safe'. But we can feel the difference. We can feel that we are restricted. There's something trying to get out. We still pick up the guitar, quietly, when no one else is in the house. We still daydream... of writing, of singing, of leading, of our business, of the freedom, expression and creativity we know is within us.

And sometimes, we realise that this self-doubt, this fear, isn't true either. Or, if it is true, we realise that we have to do the thing anyway. And we decide to dance the dance with Resistance here, too.

Again, it comes through discipline. It's through forming a habit which says something like, 'Ah, that isn't necessarily true. It's just Resistance. I need to carry on. I need to *do the work.*'

But then, if we're dancing here, maybe Resistance gets us some other way. Often it ties us in knots.

I can't coach more clients until I've done more coaching. Or, *the financial pressure is just too high for me to go to these sales meetings. I can't do it.* Or, *I don't want to get this business idea going in case someone else takes it.* (Even though your previous ideas were done by others first, because you didn't act on them). Or, *I don't make time to do creative work because I don't know what I'd do with it.* (Even though the only way you'll really know is to give yourself time to create).

These last two are me.

The last one is me *now*.

Resistance is everywhere, it's devious, and it's not going away. If Paulo Coelho still has to schedule in hours each day for procrastination, just to make sure he gets to *the work*, then we probably need to take steps too.

Why is this important?

It's important because today, contributing to the world is easier than ever before. Anyone with a smartphone or access to an internet café can contribute to making the world a better place. By sharing their art, whatever that may be. By starting a business that truly serves people, making their lives better. By following the deeper instinct inside them, that knows where they should really be.

Because it's a part of the great dance, the great pattern. Because people might be inspired. They might be changed for the better. Happier, because of what you did. And here's the true secret, and maybe the reason you're scared to do it: you will be happier, too.

Almost all the gatekeepers are gone. You don't need a publisher. You don't need a record label. You don't need a production company. You don't need a bank loan. You need £100 (or less) and internet access.

And you need to be able to dance with your Resistance. It won't be easy, but you can do it. Because many have before.

Don't be one of those who stopped the dance and didn't start again; who gave up and left relics of art which might have changed the world inside cupboards or inside heads.

The dance won't be easy, but it will change you. And it will change the world.

Come dance with us.

Afterword

Written on 24th August, 2021

And then, all of a sudden, here we are at the end. The end of the start.

As I write this, six years or so into my work as a coach, five years and one week into this 12-minute writing practice, three themes are emerging that I believe will be threaded throughout the next phase of my work.

One of those threads is the coaching I do with leaders, entrepreneurs and others who want to make a big difference in the world we live in. Often this work happens when the question is asked: how do I succeed in even more extraordinary ways, without compromising who I am? How do I get ahead without having to 'play the game', just by being me more, with skill? How do I lead with honour?

Another thread is supporting and developing the craft of coaching, which I believe has such an important part to play in the next phase of humanity, supporting, as it does, people to be their most skilful, noble, wise selves. Only when we are our most skilful, noble, wise selves can we be sure that we are doing our absolute best to make things better and not worse.

But perhaps the most important is the third thread. The one that this book is about: how do we actually *do* the important things. When it feels impossible, when it feels all struggle and no reward, when it is hard, when we haven't done it for years, even though on some level we want to.

That's what the leaders I coach are often struggling with when they want to begin to change the culture of their organisation for the better, to develop their skills so they can be more effective, to start their business so they can have an impact, to be the leader they want to be.

That's what coaches I support are struggling with as they try to make their practices work, as they face down their fears to be public about the work they love, as they take the steps to make their work even more powerful.

And that's what this book, and the sequels that follow it, are about. How do we actually *do* the important things?

I hope that, now you have read this book, you have more answers to that question. For *you*.

I hope that you are more equipped to step out into the world and start something. Something important. Something that will change you – because creating things *will* change you – and something that will change others. Something that will make this world a little more like the heaven it could be.

The first part of that is to start.

That's not the last part. As Brandon Sanderson wrote in *Oathbringer*, the most important step a person can take is not the first, but the next. The most important step is always the next one.

But worry about that later, because the first next step is the first step. It is the start.

For today, let's get started.

Help Spread the Word

I believe that the world is a better place when people are creating things; when people move out of the hell of procrastination and create things that make a difference.

If you agree with me, or if this book has helped you, please help someone else start when they're stuck by doing one of two things:

1. Review this book on Amazon

It really can't be overstated how important reviews are to help a book reach the people it's intended to help. If you have taken something positive from reading this book, please spare five minutes of your time to help someone else find their something positive too. You never know where it might take them.

Even just a few words will make a big difference.

2. Tell someone about this book

Do you know someone who always talks about the book they'll write or the business they'll start or the creative project they've just thought of… but they never start?

If you do, tell them about this book. Tell them the story of how I wrote it. Give it to them for their birthday or for Christmas. It might be exactly what they need.

Please Share Your Work: Free E-book

If you want to make a difference, you *have* to start.

And if you want to make a difference, at some point your work has to connect to someone else. I want your work to make a difference and that's why I'm giving you a draft copy of the fourth book in the 12-Minute Method series *for free*.

To get your copy visit

www.robbieswale.com/12minute-method-downloads

This book, provisionally titled *How to Share Your Work Even When You're Scared*, contains more practical inspiration aimed at getting your idea off the ground and out into the world.

The full book will be published in 2022, but this draft version will always be free to you via the above link.

Stay Up to Date About The 12-Minute Method

This is the first in a series of books, created to support you through the creative process. The next three books in the series will be published in 2022.

To be the first to hear about those books, other exciting 12-Minute Method developments, and my other work, sign up to my mailing list at:

www.robbieswale.com/mailing-list

Acknowledgments

Written on 22nd October, 2021

I recommend to every author that they write their acknowledgments with a 12-minute timer, as it occurs to me that this gives me the perfect excuse if I forget someone.

Thank you, first of all, to the people who have practically worked on this book: Steve Creek for that first copy edit, and more importantly for the conversation in a coffee shop and the challenge to make the book as a whole what the prospective title promised. That, undoubtedly, led us here. Thanks also to Tim Pettingale and Joseph Alexander at **www.self-published.co.uk**. I was trying to find the perfect partners to help me get this book out, and your energy, passion, generosity and integrity made you those people. Thanks also to those like Stefan at Spiffing Covers who worked on this book as part of your team.

Thank you to all the giants on whose shoulders this book stands. I've tried to credit the writers and thinkers whose ideas have influenced me wherever they have cropped up, but I'm sure I've missed some or made mistakes in some places. I'm sorry about that – and I don't even have the '12 minutes' excuse there anymore.

A pride of place acknowledgement should go to the coaches and mentors who have supported me over the years from the start of the 12-minute practice through to the publication of this book. That includes Mike Toller, Rich Litvin, Katie Harvey, Robert Holden and more. Their influence is present in this book, sometimes explicitly and often implicitly. And, most of all, to Joel Monk – for that tiny part of a conversation in a coaching session in 2016 where 'the train series' began. I can feel tears tingling my eyes and nose writing this. Wow. What impact we created together in that moment, rippling down the years and out into the world. The still moment where so much turned. Thank you, Joel, for that moment of magic and inspiration and leadership and presence. Look what we made! And this is just the start.

Thank you to everyone who has read a 12-minute article, and special thanks to those who have liked, shared and commented on (online and in person) those articles. If no one had done that, particularly on the first ones, this book wouldn't be here. Supporting the creativity of others can have untold impact; thank you to everyone who has supported mine.

And thank you, of course, to those people who are closest to me, who have helped me become who I am. My wife, Emma; my mum, dad, brother and sister. My close friends.

And, also, to my daughter Leah, currently 10 months old and a well of joy and love. It is often necessary that I tell her, 'Swales don't eat books!' But Swales do, it turns out, write them.

Lastly, thank you, whoever you are, for reading. And thank you for what you create.

How I Wrote a Book in 12 Minutes: Notes About the Process

For those who are interested, I wanted to add a few words about how this book was created, and the idea of creating a book in 12 minutes, to supplement what I described in the introduction and throughout the book. I share this to give those among you who want to do something similar the power to choose how you do that.

I imagined originally that this series (this book and the ones that will follow) would simply be a compilation of the pieces as they were posted online, but once something starts to become a book, some extra decisions need to be made.

First, it felt important to give myself a little more leeway than I do with the articles when they first go online. I gave myself an extra proofread/edit of the whole book, then I sent it to my friend, Steve Creek, a professional copy editor, to give it a once over.

The spirit of those edits was to improve it, so it could support people even more. It was to tighten and clarify. The substance of the articles was not changed significantly – a sentence was added or removed here and there, a few titles made more relevant or punchier. There were a few tweaks to make the language and sense clearer, or to fix bits that were hazy on detail because the original was written in 12 minutes and there wasn't time to look up precisely what someone had said. After the book came back from Steve, there was some broader feedback and some rearranging of the pieces, then it sat, pretty much untouched, for about two years (more on that another time).

When I came back to it, with the help of Tim Pettingale and Joseph Alexander from **www.self-published.co.uk**, we realised it would work even better as a series, but that required another edit from me, again leaving the substance but tightening and making clearer a sentence here and there, or adding a few words to make it clear why a particular piece belonged here, in this part of the series. As the publishing process went on, the book received an edit from Tim and another two reads and light edits from me. I noticed, as each time passed, that I was more willing to tweak for clarity and impact. But, as you can tell from reading, these pieces are absolutely imperfect, and many are pretty much exactly as they were originally written on the train or with the 12-minute timer.

At different stages, I also added in introductions to each part, to help tie the book together. Those introductions, the notes and pages about free gifts, and this piece are the only bits not originally written in 12 minutes, although even with the introductions, which mostly didn't take 12 minutes, I set the timer to make sure I got out of my own way and got going. That's how I work. The 12-Minute Method section at the start was written in the same spirit, but I had to reset the timer three times to have time to say everything that needed saying (The 36-Minute Method!).

A few pieces from the series of articles didn't quite belong in a series about creating what you are called to create, so those were removed. Remarkably few pieces from the first three years of the writing practice overlapped in content enough that a piece needed to be removed, but there were a couple, so they came out. I felt that a few more didn't help the flow of the books, so they came out too. This process was surprisingly hard, but it served the books to remove them. All these pieces can be read on LinkedIn where they were originally posted or in The Cutting Room, a short ebook available at:

www.robbieswale.com/12minute-method-downloads

I wasn't sure where to draw the line with which set of 12-minute articles would make up the series, but on my deadline to send the book to Steve, I realised it was three years and one day since I started the weekly practice (after the initial five pieces). So, what makes up this book and its three sequels are the five original parts of The Train Series and almost exactly three years of weekly articles.

And that, pretty much, is how you write a book (or four!) in 12 minutes.